H

$\triangleleft$ **W9-AQK-676**

Isaac Asimov's

21st Century

Library of the Universe

The Solar System

Pluto and Charon

BY ISAAC ASIMOV

WITH REVISIONS AND UPDATING BY RICHARD HANTULA

Gareth Stevens Publishing
A WORLD ALMANAC EDUCATION GROUP COMPANY

Please visit our web site at: www.garethstevens.com
For a free color catalog describing Gareth Stevens Publishing's list of high-quality
books and multimedia programs, call 1-800-542-2595 (USA) or 1-800-387-3178 (Canada).
Gareth Stevens Publishing's fax: (414) 332-3567.

Library of Congress Cataloging-in-Publication Data

Asimov, Isaac.
    Pluto and Charon / by Isaac Asimov; with revisions and updating by Richard Hantula.
       p. cm. — (Isaac Asimov's 21st century library of the universe. The solar system)
    Rev. ed. of: A double planet?: Pluto and Charon. 1996.
    Summary: Introduces the smallest known planet in the solar system as well as its moon.
    Includes bibliographical references and index.
    ISBN 0-8368-3240-X (lib. bdg.)
    1. Pluto (Planet)—Juvenile literature. 2. Charon (Satellite)—Juvenile literature. [1. Pluto (Planet).
2. Charon (Satellite).] I. Hantula, Richard. II. Asimov, Isaac. Double planet?: Pluto and Charon.
III. Title. IV. Isaac Asimov's 21st century library of the universe. Solar system.
QB701.A86   2002
523.48'2—dc21   2002021683

This edition first published in 2002 by
Gareth Stevens Publishing
A World Almanac Education Group Company
330 West Olive Street, Suite 100
Milwaukee, WI 53212 USA

Revised and updated edition © 2002 by Gareth Stevens, Inc. Original edition published in 1990
by Gareth Stevens, Inc. under the title *Pluto: A Double Planet?*. Second edition published in
1996 by Gareth Stevens, Inc. under the title *A Double Planet?: Pluto and Charon*. Text © 2002
by Nightfall, Inc. End matter and revisions © 2002 by Gareth Stevens, Inc.

Series editor: Betsy Rasmussen
Cover design and layout adaptation: Melissa Valuch
Picture research: Matthew Groshek
Additional picture research: Diane Laska-Swanke
Production director: Susan Ashley

The editors at Gareth Stevens Publishing have selected science author Richard Hantula to bring
this classic series of young people's information books up to date. Richard Hantula has written
and edited books and articles on science and technology for more than two decades. He was
the senior U.S. editor for the *Macmillan Encyclopedia of Science*.

In addition to Hantula's contribution to this most recent edition, the editors would like to
acknowledge the participation of two noted science authors, Greg Walz-Chojnacki and
Francis Reddy, as contributors to earlier editions of this work.

Printed in the United States of America

1 2 3 4 5 6 7 8 9 06 05 04 03 02

Contents

We live in an enormously large place – the Universe. It is only natural that we would want to understand this place, so scientists and engineers have developed instruments and spacecrafts that have told us far more about the Universe than we could possibly imagine.

We have seen planets up close, and spacecrafts have even landed on some. We have learned about quasars and pulsars, supernovas and colliding galaxies, and black holes and dark matter. We have gathered amazing data about how the Universe may have come into being and how it may end. Nothing could be more astonishing.

The most mysterious known planet in our Solar System is Pluto. Pluto is so small that some astronomers think it should be called a big asteroid rather than a planet. It is the hardest of the planets to reach and is the only one that has not been viewed close-up by a space probe. It travels in an unusual orbit around the Sun. Most of the time, it is the most distant planet in the Solar System. The rest of the time, it is the second-most distant. Scientists are gradually uncovering Pluto's mysteries.

Pluto & Charon

Distant and Undiscovered

Pluto was the last of the known planets in our Solar System to be discovered. As recently as the 1920s, the two farthest known planets were Uranus and Neptune.

Astronomers could determine some facts about Uranus and Neptune, such as the planets' orbits around the Sun. Even when astronomers considered the gravitational pull of every known planet, however, they could not completely explain certain unusual wobbly motions that Uranus and Neptune seemed to make. Could there be an undiscovered planet farther out that was pulling on Uranus and Neptune?

Astronomers watched the sky to see if they could find a new, distant planet.

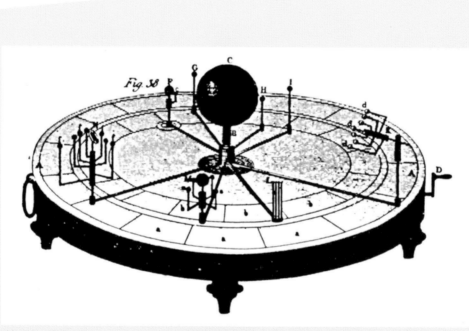

Above: This historic drawing depicts what is known as an orrery, a mechanical model of the Solar System. This orrery does not contain Neptune and Pluto, because they were not yet discovered when the orrery was made.

Like dancers in a celestial ballet, the planets circle our Sun, held in orbit by the Sun's gravitational pull. The gravity of each planet also pulls a little at every other planet.

Pluto Appears

Astronomer Percival Lowell built the Lowell Observatory in Arizona in 1894. There, he searched for a possible new planet. He calculated where it ought to be to create a pull on Uranus and Neptune, but he did not find it.

After Lowell's death in 1916, an astronomer named Clyde Tombaugh continued the mission at Lowell Observatory.

Tombaugh took photographs of particular parts of the sky on different nights. He used a device that showed one photo and then another in rapid succession. With this method, the stars would not appear to move but a planet would.

On February 18, 1930, Tombaugh came up with a pair of photographs in which a dot moved. The moving dot was Pluto.

Right: Pluto, the ancient Roman god of the underworld.

Name that planet!

Many celestial bodies are named for characters in Greek and Roman myths. When Pluto was discovered, an 11-year-old English schoolgirl, Venetia Burney, stated that the new planet was so far from the Sun that it must get only dim light, so it should be named Pluto — for the Roman god of the underworld. The suggestion was accepted by scientists. As an added bonus, the first two letters, PL, memorialized Percival Lowell, who built the observatory from where Pluto was detected.

Above: Astronomer Clyde Tombaugh found Pluto in 1930 after viewing hundreds of photographs.

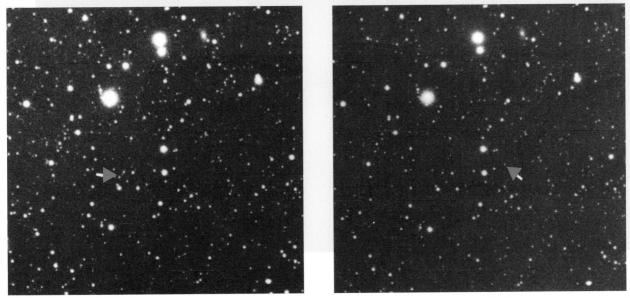

Above: The first photos of Pluto. These pictures, taken about a week apart, show that one dot *(see arrows)* has moved — the planet Pluto.

Pluto is made of rock with a coating of ice. A thin outer layer contains frozen methane, nitrogen, and carbon monoxide.

Coming Full Circle

Pluto is nearly 3.7 billion miles (5.9 billion kilometers) from the Sun, on average. This is about 40 times as far from the Sun as Earth is. This means that to go around the Sun just once, Pluto has to travel along an orbit 40 times as long as Earth's orbit.

At Pluto's great distance, the Sun's gravity is so weak that

Pluto moves only $^1/_6$ as fast around the Sun as Earth does. Pluto takes about 248 Earth years to travel around the Sun because of its long orbit and slow speed.

Not until the year 2178 will Pluto finally be back at the place in the sky where it was discovered in 1930.

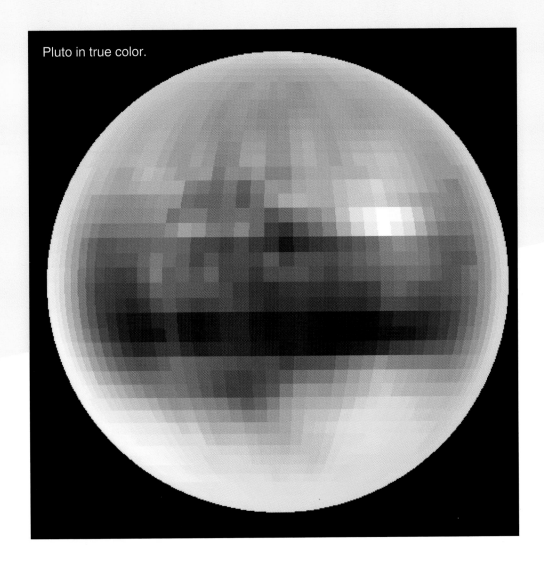

Pluto in true color.

Lopsided Travels

The planets do not travel around the Sun in perfect circles, but in slightly lopsided or egg-shaped orbits. These types of orbits are called elliptical. A planet in an elliptical orbit is a little closer to the Sun at one end of its orbit than at the other.

Pluto's orbit is quite lopsided. At its farthest, Pluto is about 4.6 billion miles (7.4 billion km) away from the Sun. At its closest, it is only 2.7 billion miles (4.4 billion km) away from the Sun. When at its closest, Pluto is a little nearer to the Sun than Neptune is. Pluto and Neptune do not collide, because Pluto's orbit is tilted. Also, Pluto is sometimes above Neptune's orbit and sometimes below it. The two planets never come closer than roughly 1.6 billion miles (2.5 billion km) from each other.

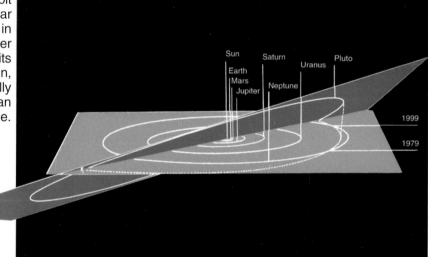

Right: Pluto's orbit takes the planet far from the plane in which the other planets orbit. At its closest to the Sun, Pluto is actually closer than Neptune.

The origins of Pluto — a cosmic escapee?

Could Pluto once have been a moon of Neptune? It is no bigger than a middle-sized moon, and due to its lopsided orbit, it moves in closer to the Sun than Neptune does. So some astronomers thought it might once have been a satellite of Neptune that got knocked away in some cosmic catastrophe. Scientists have traced Pluto's orbit back in time, however, and it does not seem that the planet was ever close enough to Neptune to have been its satellite.

Is Pluto an escaped moon of Neptune? It is an interesting thought, but scientists are doubtful that Pluto ever orbited Neptune. This picture shows an artist's conception of Pluto *(front)* revolving around blue Neptune.

A Double Planet?

Between 1979 and 1999, Pluto was closer to the Sun than Neptune was. Pluto could also be seen better at this time than at any other time.

In 1978, astronomer James W. Christy noticed a bulge on a photograph he had taken of Pluto. He looked at earlier photos and found the bulge in different spots. In this way, Christy discovered that Pluto has a moon moving around it. He named the moon Charon (pronounced Sharon) after his wife Char. By coincidence, in Greek mythology, the boatman who transported spirits to the underworld — the realm of the god Pluto — is also named Charon (pronounced KAIR-on).

Charon is a little more than $1/2$ as wide as Pluto. No other known planet has a satellite that similar to it in size. This means that Pluto is practically a double planet. Only Earth and its Moon, which is about $1/4$ the width of Earth, come almost as close to being a double planet.

This picture showed astronomer James Christy that Pluto has a moon. The bulge *(right)* appears in different places in other pictures.

Earth to Pluto!

Most moons are much smaller than their parent planets. Ganymede, the biggest moon in our Solar System, has only about $1/12,000$ the mass of Jupiter. Titan, the Solar System's second biggest moon, has just $1/4,000$ of Saturn's mass. Our Moon, however, has $1/80$ the mass of Earth. Until the discovery of Charon, the combination of Earth and our Moon was the closest thing to a double planet in the Solar System. Then scientists found that Charon has about $1/8$ the mass of Pluto. Pluto and Charon are much smaller than Earth and its Moon, but they are a great deal closer to being a double planet.

An artist's conception of the formation of Pluto and Charon from the rocky debris at the edge of the Solar System.

Charon, boatman of the underworld in ancient Greek myths.

13

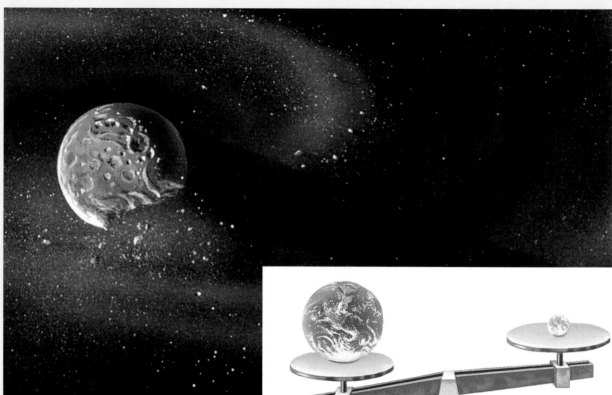

Above: According to one theory, Charon formed from a cloud of debris created when an asteroid or comet collided with Pluto long ago.

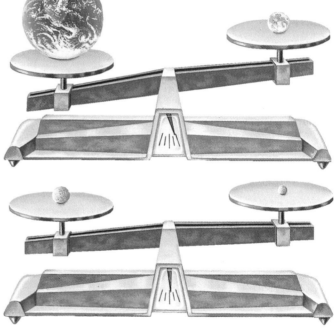

Right: Earth is 80 times more massive than our Moon *(top scale)*. Pluto is just 8 times more massive than its moon, Charon *(bottom scale)*.

The origins of Charon — a chip off the old block?

Why should Pluto have so large a moon? Giant planets sometimes capture small objects that wander too closely to them. Pluto is far too small to capture anything the size of Charon, however. Pluto and Charon may once have been a single body that somehow broke apart. That would explain why they are separated by only about 12,200 miles (19,600 km) — roughly $1/20$ the distance between Earth and the Moon. What would have caused the original planet to break up? Scientists do not know.

Small Worlds After All

When astronomers first searched for Pluto, they thought it would have to be fairly large to pull strongly on Neptune and Uranus. Pluto turned out to be much smaller than expected. It was difficult, however, for astronomers to say exactly how small Pluto was, because they could not see it well enough through telescopes on Earth. Charon was even more difficult to see.

Finally, in the 1980s, astronomers made progress by measuring how long stars remained hidden when Pluto or Charon moved in front of them. Astronomers also got helpful data by studying what happened when Charon passed in front of Pluto and vice versa. Also of help were pictures of Pluto made by the Hubble Space Telescope in the 1990s. Astronomers calculated that Pluto was about 1,430 miles (2,300 km) across – smaller than Earth's Moon. In fact, Pluto weighs only about 1/5 as much as our Moon. Charon is only about 750 miles (1,200 km) across and weighs only 1/8 as much as Pluto.

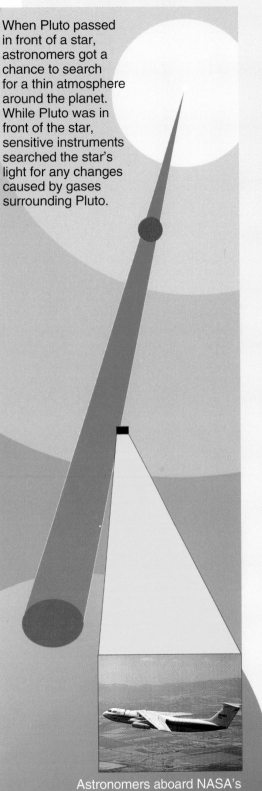

When Pluto passed in front of a star, astronomers got a chance to search for a thin atmosphere around the planet. While Pluto was in front of the star, sensitive instruments searched the star's light for any changes caused by gases surrounding Pluto.

Astronomers aboard NASA's *Kuiper Airborne Observatory*, a telescope-equipped jet plane named for astronomer Gerard Kuiper, were the first to detect Pluto's thin atmosphere.

Uncovering Pluto

Despite its small size and great distance from Earth, astronomers have managed to discover some details about Pluto.

In the 1950s, astronomers found that Pluto's light grew slightly brighter every 6.4 days. They realized this was because Pluto turned on its axis in that time, showing first a brighter side and then a dimmer side as it turned.

Beginning in the late 1970s, astronomers learned much about Pluto's surface by analyzing light reflected from it. They discovered that it was covered with ice made partly of frozen methane, a chemical found in natural gas on Earth. Astronomers also found signs of frozen nitrogen and carbon monoxide.

Above: According to one theory, during summertime on Pluto, frozen methane and other frozen chemicals on the planet's surface turn into gas and create an atmosphere. Darker material beneath the ice then becomes visible *(left)*. During winter, the gases in the atmosphere freeze and brighten Pluto with a fresh coat of frost *(right)*.

On Earth, pockets of methane accompany oil deep underground. Here, an oil refinery burns off excess methane.

Sharing the Atmosphere

When Pluto's orbit brings it nearest Earth, Charon moves in front of and then behind Pluto every 6.4 days.

Charon is darker than Pluto. By studying light reflected from Charon, astronomers have found that Charon has little or no methane on its surface but probably does have ice made from water.

The temperature at Pluto's surface ranges from about -350° Fahrenheit (-210° Centigrade) down to -390° F (-235° C).

Pluto is big enough and cold enough that it is able to have a thin atmosphere of nitrogen, methane, and other gases.

Charon probably has no atmosphere of its own, because it is smaller than Pluto and has less gravity. Pluto and Charon are so close in distance, however, that particles in Pluto's atmosphere may extend out to Charon. In a way, you could say that the Pluto-Charon system may be a double planet enclosed in a single atmosphere.

Right: Diagram of Charon's orbit in relation to Pluto.

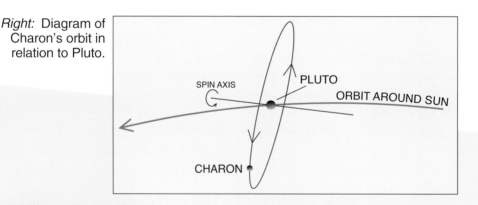

SPIN AXIS

PLUTO

ORBIT AROUND SUN

CHARON

Pluto and Charon — a cosmic face-off!

When a small celestial body circles a larger one, its rotation is slowed by tides. This is why a moon faces only one side to its planet — its speed of rotation has been slowed down. Earth's Moon, for example, faces only one side to Earth. A moon also produces a slowing effect on the planet it circles, but the planet is usually so much larger and more massive than the moon that its rotation slows just slightly. In the case of Pluto and Charon, however, the two bodies are so nearly equal in size that each faces the same side to each other.

If you were standing on Charon during one of its eclipses of Pluto, you could watch the dark shadow of Charon sweep across the frozen surface of Pluto.

Ice crystals in Pluto's atmosphere create a rare arc of light around the distant Sun. It is the beginning of Pluto's long winter, and frost has started to coat the planet's surface as the atmosphere freezes.

Starry Days and Nights

The Sun looks quite different from Pluto than it does from Earth, because Pluto is so much farther from the Sun. Viewing the Sun from Pluto, you might think of the Sun as just another star. Even when Pluto is at its closest to the Sun, it gets only about $1/900$ as much sunlight as Earth gets. No wonder Pluto is so cold.

Still, from distant Pluto, the Sun looks 1,000 times brighter than the full Moon looks when viewed from Earth, because Pluto's thin atmosphere does not scatter sunlight the way Earth's atmosphere does. Stars are visible from Pluto even with the Sun in the sky.

From Pluto, the Sun is still 14 million times brighter than any other star. After all, the next nearest star is thousands of times farther away than the Sun.

In the 22nd century,
humans may view Pluto
and Charon in person as
interplanetary visitors.

Still Unexplored

So far, spacecrafts have explored all the planets except one – Pluto. One scientist calls Pluto the "Mount Everest" of Solar System exploration, because it is the most distant, the coldest, and the hardest planet to reach.

NASA has considered sending a probe to take pictures and gather data in the outer parts of the Solar System. Under one plan, such a probe would reach Pluto as early as the year 2015.

In the meantime, the Hubble Space Telescope has taken excellent pictures of Pluto and its companion, Charon. Scientists are combining new data with what they already know to improve their knowledge of Pluto and Charon.

Left: Pluto and Charon showing hints of surface features, taken by the Hubble Space Telescope with the ESA Faint Object Camera in late June and early July 1994.

An image of Pluto and Charon taken by the Hubble Space Telescope using the ESA's Faint Object Camera in February 1994.

In 1983, the Infrared Astronomical Satellite (IRAS), a telescope sensitive to heat, searched the entire sky for objects too cool to glow by their own light — such as a tenth planet — and none was found.

A Tenth Planet?

Pluto was found while searching for a planet whose gravity was tugging at Uranus and Neptune. Scientists realized, however, that Pluto's gravity is too weak to make that kind of difference. For that reason, many people searched for a tenth planet beyond Pluto. Such a planet would have to have enough gravity to make Uranus and Neptune follow the slightly wobbly orbits that they seemed to have. More recently, though, astronomers decided that Uranus and Neptune do not really wobble after all. They believe that early observations of these planets are not reliable. The proof lies in the fact that spacecrafts have successfully been sent to Uranus and Neptune using calculations that were not based on early observations.

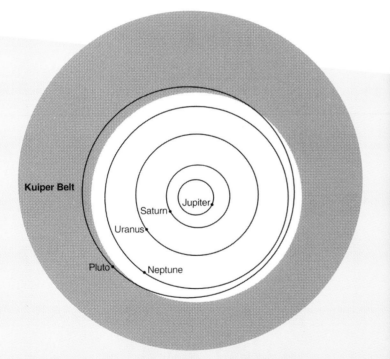

Above: Pluto has an odd orbit like the recently discovered asteroids in the Kuiper Belt. More and more of these objects are being found all the time. Perhaps a new "Pluto" will be among them.

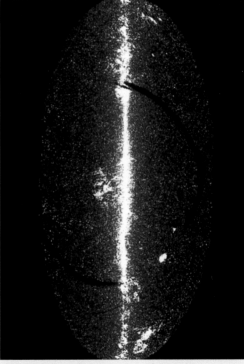

Above: An infrared map of the sky. The bright band is the Milky Way.

Is Pluto Really a Planet?

Pluto's small size and lopsided orbit cause many people to wonder whether Pluto should be considered a planet at all. Some other bodies in the Solar System have orbits similar to Pluto's, and seven moons of other planets are larger than Pluto. Some people have said that since Pluto has a moon it must be a planet; but astronomers have discovered that some asteroids have moons, too.

Scientists have also learned that thousands of small objects travel around the Sun beyond Neptune in a region of space called the Kuiper Belt. Many astronomers think that Pluto is just one of the largest of these objects and that Neptune is the farthest "real" planet.

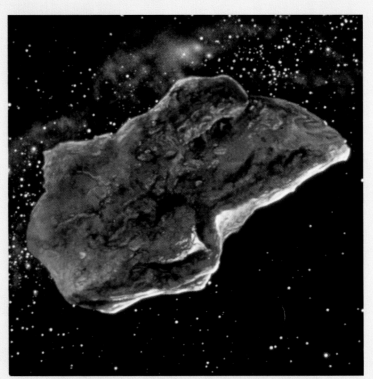

Above: A comet in orbit far from the Sun in a collection of comets called the Oort Cloud. Just like planets and asteroids, comets may also have moons.

The Oort Comet Cloud.

The Sun and its Solar System family (*left to right*): Mercury, Venus, Earth, Mars, Jupiter, Saturn, Uranus, Neptune, Pluto.

Fact File: Pluto's Secrets Revealed

Pluto is our Solar System's smallest known planet. It also is, for most of its orbit, the farthest from the Sun. It takes the longest of any known planet to orbit the Sun — nearly 248 Earth years.

Tiny Pluto is still revealing its secrets to astronomers. One of Pluto's most exciting aspects — the existence of its moon, Charon — came to light in 1978. Charon lies very close to its companion planet and is not much smaller in size and mass. Pluto and Charon seem to be almost a double planet. Some astronomers believe that the two may even share the same atmosphere.

Four other planets — Jupiter, Saturn, Neptune, and Earth — have moons that are bigger than Pluto. In the minds of some astronomers, tiny Pluto barely qualifies as a planet at all.

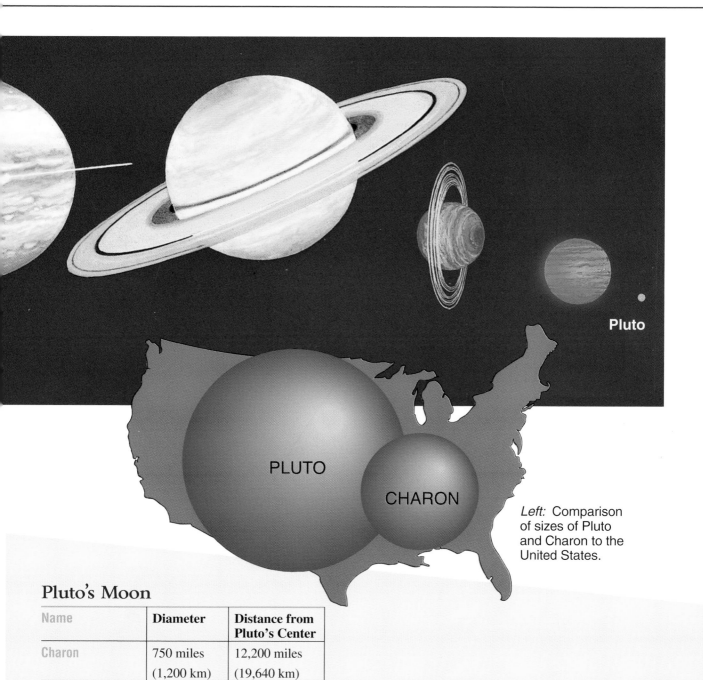

Pluto

Left: Comparison of sizes of Pluto and Charon to the United States.

Pluto's Moon

Name	Diameter	Distance from Pluto's Center
Charon	750 miles (1,200 km)	12,200 miles (19,640 km)

Pluto: How it measures up to Earth

Planet	Diameter	Rotation Period (length of day)	Period of Orbit around Sun (length of year)	Moons	Surface Gravity	Distance from Sun (nearest–farthest)	Least Time It Takes for Light to Reach Earth
Pluto	1,430 miles (2,300 km)	6 days, 9 hours, 18 minutes	247.7 years	1	0.06*	2.7–4.6 billion miles (4.4–7.4 billion km)	3.9 hours —
Earth	7,927 miles (12,756 km)	23 hours, 56 minutes	365.25 days (1 year)	1	1.0*	91–94 million miles (147–152 million km)	— —

* Multiply your weight by this number to find out how much you would weigh on this planet.

More Books about Pluto

Clyde Tombaugh and the Search for Planet X. Margaret K. Wetterer (Carolrhoda Books)

DK Space Encyclopedia. Nigel Henbest and Heather Couper (DK Publishing)

The Outer Planets: Uranus, Neptune, and Pluto. Giles Sparrow (Heinemann Library)

Pluto. Carmen Bredeson (Franklin Watts)

Pluto and the Search for New Planets. Gregory Vogt (Raintree Steck-Vaughn)

CD-ROMs

Exploring the Planets. (Cinegram)

Web Sites

The Internet is a good place to get more information about Pluto. The web sites listed here can help you learn about the most recent discoveries, as well as those made in the past.

KidsAstronomy. www.kidsastronomy.com

Nine Planets. www.nineplanets.org/pluto.html

StarDate Online. stardate.org/resources/ssguide/pluto.html

Views of the Solar System. www.solarviews.com/eng/pluto.htm

Windows to the Universe. www.windows.ucar.edu/tour/link=/pluto/pluto.html

Places to Visit

Here are some museums and centers where you can find a variety of space exhibits.

American Museum of Natural History
Central Park West at 79th Street
New York, NY 10024

Boston Museum of Science
Science Park
Boston, MA 02114

Canada Science and Technology Museum
1867 St. Laurent Boulevard
100 Queen's Park
Ottawa, Ontario K1G5A3
Canada

National Air and Space Museum
Smithsonian Institution
7th and Independence Avenue SW
Washington, DC 20560

Odyssium
11211 142nd Street
Edmonton, Alberta T5M 4A1
Canada

Scienceworks Museum
2 Booker Street
Spotswood
Melbourne, Victoria 3015
Australia

Glossary

asteroids: very small "planets." Hundreds of thousands of them exist in our Solar System. Most of them orbit the Sun between Mars and Jupiter, but many occur elsewhere.

atmosphere: gases surrounding a planet, star, or moon.

axis: the imaginary straight line around which a planet, star, or moon turns or rotates.

carbon monoxide: a colorless, odorless gas containing carbon and oxygen.

comet: an object in space made of ice, rock, and gas. It has a vapor tail that can be seen from Earth when the comet's orbit brings it close to the Sun.

double planet: two planets that circle each other.

eclipse: the partial or complete blocking of light from one astronomical body by another.

elliptical: oval in shape.

ESA: European Space Agency.

gravity: the force that causes objects like Earth and the Moon to be attracted to one another.

Hubble Space Telescope: an artificial satellite containing a telescope and related instruments that was placed in orbit around Earth in 1990.

Kuiper Belt: small bodies in the region of the Solar System lying beyond Neptune. They seem to mostly resemble icy comets, but some may be rocky asteroids.

mass: the amount of matter that an object contains.

methane gas: a colorless, odorless, flammable gas.

moon: a small body in space that moves in an orbit around a larger body. A moon is said to be a satellite of the larger body.

nitrogen: a chemical element that at sufficiently warm temperatures occurs as a colorless, odorless gas. It is found in the atmospheres of Earth and Pluto.

Oort Cloud: a grouping of comets surrounding the Solar System. It is named after the Dutch astronomer Jan Oort, who suggested its existence in 1950.

orbit: the path that one celestial object follows as it circles or revolves around another.

probe: a craft that travels in space, photographing and studying celestial bodies and in some cases even landing on them.

Solar System: our Sun with the planets and all the other bodies, such as asteroids, that orbit the Sun.

Sun: our star and the provider of energy that makes life possible on Earth.

Tombaugh, Clyde: the American astronomer who discovered Pluto in 1930.

underworld: in ancient Greek and Roman mythology, the place where it was believed people went when they died.

Index

Born in 1920, Isaac Asimov came to the United States as a young boy from his native Russia. As a young man, he was a student of biochemistry. In time, he became one of the most productive writers the world has ever known. His books cover a spectrum of topics, including science, history, language theory, fantasy, and science fiction. His brilliant imagination gained him the respect and admiration of adults and children alike. Sadly, Isaac Asimov died shortly after the publication of the first edition of *Isaac Asimov's Library of the Universe.*

The publishers wish to thank the following for permission to reproduce copyright material: front cover, 3, NASA; 4, copyright-free reproduction from Heck, J. G., *The Complete Encyclopedia of Illustration*; 5, © Rick Karpinski/DeWalt and Associates 1989; 6, © Keith Ward 1989; 7 (all), Lowell Observatory; 8, © Lynette Cook 1989; 9, Courtesy of Southwest Research Institute; 10, © Sally Bensusen 1982; 11, © Paul Dimare 1989; 12, U.S. Navy; 13 (large), © Michael Carroll 1989; 13 (inset), © Keith Ward 1989; 14 (upper), © Michael Carroll 1989; 14 (lower), © Lynette Cook 1989; 15 (large), Kate Kriege/© Gareth Stevens, Inc.; 15 (inset), NASA; 16 (both), © Paul Dimare 1989; 17, © Stewart M. Green/Tom Stack and Associates; 18, Fran Bagenal & Steve Bartlett; 19, © Joe Shabram 1987; 20-21, © John Foster 1985; 22, © Pat Rawlings 1989; 23 (upper), NASA; 23 (lower), National Space Science Data Center; 24, Jet Propulsion Laboratory; 25 (left), © Gareth Stevens, Inc.; 25 (right), Jet Propulsion Laboratory; 26, © Michael Carroll; 27, © Calvin J. Hamilton; 28-29, © Sally Bensusen 1987; 29, Fran Bagenal & Steve Bartlett.